FROM THE HORNS OF THE BULL OF THE BULL TO THE USA

HECTOR ESPINOSA

outskirtspress

DENVER, COLORADO

Outskirts Press, Inc.
http://www.outskirtspress.com

ISBN: 978-1-4787-4639-3

Outskirts Press and the "OP" logo are trademarks belonging to Outskirts Press, Inc.

PRINTED IN THE UNITED STATES OF AMERICA

Table of Contents

s b
ne
r

CHILDHOOD YEARS

1943 to 1954

I was born on October 12 1940 in the village of Solana about 4 miles from the town of Macheta, Colombia. My father Juan de Jesus Espinosa and my mother Romelia Espinosa were born in 1913. They dedicated themselves to agriculture as it is the norm with the majority of the Colombian population. Based on my vague recollection my father's great grandfather emigrated from Spain who settled in the Village of Solana. From my mother's side her father and mother also had her roots from Spain. His ancestry was not clearly defined however because his features were mixed with those of the native Indians of the locality.

My father's education was limited to be able to read and write. He was a very curious man and was abreast of the news not only about Colombia but of the whole world. My mother, on the other hand, did not know how to write but was able to read rather well. I recalled that as part of our faith before bedtime, she routinely read the mysteries while praying the rosary and on Easter season she read the passion of our lord.

My father was a disciplinarian with us in all respects. He taught us good manners like addressing to other people by his or last name and never to show anyone any form of disrespect. He emphatically said to us that: "To be respected, you must respect others first." His teaching words were spoken with finality and were ingrained permanently within us.

As a young boy of about 4 years of age I remember my father's father Nicacio Espinosa a man of short stature of white sideburns, short mustache, and a reddish complexion that made him stand out from the locals. I also vividly remembered when our father built the first house of mud and straw on land gifted from my mother's father. It was fun time for me to mix the mud with the straw and splash it onto the wall. The house had two rooms. One room for us to sleep in, no window, so a limited amount of light entered the room unless the door was left ajar. The other room, much larger, did have a small window and was utilized mostly for storage of either potatoes or corn. The corn was stored 15 feet above the floor in the space we call today an attic supported by corn stubble bound by hemp. Needless to say, there was no protection for the corn because at night as the mice came crawling to feast on the corn the noise was somewhat scary. Many at times the number of mice was so large that there was need to have at least two mouse traps installed.

My father on occasion when the crawling and crunching of the corn by the mice, was

Loud, he would go up to the attic making noise with a belt to spook the mice away. There was no kitchen built until 2 years later. In the meantime the cooking was done on the floor of the larger room in a manner similar to that of a campsite. My grandparents' house was located a short distance from ours separated by a stream which was used as the source of running water. As one my aunts Etelvina, made her trips to carry water she would beckon me by opening her arms. At the sight of that welcoming sign I would run as fast as I could, jumping over the stream and joyfully land into her arms. Being the first born I was deeply loved by my father. He would take me wherever he had to work or simply do the daily chores in the farm. As a farmer, one of the essential needs is to own bulls to plow the fields. My father had recently purchased two bulls which he kept in a grassy field about 2 miles from the house. One sunny hot day, it was the appropriate time during midday to take the bulls to the water source. My mother had gone shopping to the town of Macheta on a Monday which is customarily the market day for the town. My father did not feel comfortable to leave me alone in the house because of my young age, I would guess between 3 and 4 years Old, so he decided to take me along with him. As he usually did, he carried me on his back to where the two bulls were tied by a rope to a stick on the ground separated far enough to prevent them from fighting. My father sat me down under a large shady tree near the fence and told me to wait there until he came back from taking the bulls to the water source. Though both bulls were tethered by rope they supposedly were tamed, he realized quickly they were very powerful. The wild instinct became obvious as soon as the rope was loosened from the stick .Because he could not take control of both animals by himself at the same time, he took the larger bull towards the stream leaving the smaller one untied in the middle of the field about 500 feet from where I was sitting. My dad felt that the bull would not cause any harm to me since it was very tame and stood at a safe distance from where I was.

Once the animal felt without the company of the other, he became nervous and gingerly began pacing towards me. He approached and stopped about 25 feet from me. I'm sitting immobile, unafraid, trusting the belief of his gentle nature I tossed a small stick with a command to go away. The bull did not move and with its eyes fixated on me, I suddenly felt a cold shiver run though my whole body. The bull was then close enough to me that I could feel the warmth air of his nostrils on my face. Suddenly, like a streak of lighting, I was hurled about 15 feet up into the air like a bundle of grass landing about 20 feet from where my father had left me. To my own disbelief I was not injured, felt no pain and did not cry. The bull immediately retreated back to where my dad left him apparently trying to cover up his mischief. Upon my father's return with the other bull, he immediately noticed that I was not sitting on the same spot. Securing the other bull, he ran to me asking me if I was okay because of the fear and pale color displayed on my face. I was speechless. He immediately suspected that the bull had charged at me and became very angry. He tied down the bull and gave it a whipping. An act that I though was futile and somewhat cruel.

My mother's parents ,Clodoveo and Francisca, also lived within walking distance on a raised plateau in a triangular shaped house with white walls and thatched roof. Like all the houses in the village of Solana. Itt did not have toilets or electricity. This house did have a small stream of water running behind the kitchen which emptied into a 3 foot deep pond where my grand- mother washed the clothes. As a matter of routine my mother paid a visit to her parents every Wednesday and I always looked forward to go with her. We had to cross 4 parcels of land 2 of which were planted with either corn or potatoes. My favorite time was walking through the cornfield because it gave me the feeling of walking in a jungle. As I looked up I marveled at the high stalks which many of them had up to 4 ears of corn. On one occasion while mother was visiting with grandmother, I slipped out of her view while I went to see the water in the pond. Like any child the fascination with water is irresistible. I found a small bucket which I wanted to fill up but the slippery soil around the pond caused me to fall into the pond. As I touched the bottom, I felt that two hands had pulled out but there was no one there. I was rescued by a miracle. I don't remember my mother ever mentioning to my father my accident.

During the next few days I began to feel a chill through my body and my appetite decreased markedly to the point I could no longer eat or swallow. Any liquid I attempted to drink would be expelled out through my nose. After 7 days I had become so weak that I could no longer stand up, my legs felt as weak as gel causing me to collapse.

My sudden illness caused my parents tremendous concern so my father decided to take me to the local medical doctor in Macheta. Not having any other manner of transportation, my father carried me on his back. The trip from Solana to Macheta is arduous because the road was not paved. It was designed for horses and mules to carry the loads of vegetables. He made it in about 1 hour. The examination by the town doctor was quick assessing that I had diphtheria and I needed immediate extensive medical care. He told my father," this boy is seriously ill, you must take him to the hospital in Bogota within 24 hours at the latest." My father's anguish for the precarious state of my health was compounded by the fact that he was not familiar with Bogota. The only possible bridge of communication was with one of his sisters who had a restaurant and could possibly give him directions. The distance from Macheta to Bogota is about 65 miles traveled by bus but it seemed that it took an eternity. After stopping at the restaurant my dad made the last attempt to feed me light soup but to no avail. I was beginning to lose my consciousness and again he carried me on his back block after block until finally we reached for the last bastion of hope, the hospital called "Hospital de La Misericordia."

It was early morning at the hospital, with the written authorization from our local doctor I was admitted without delay. The head doctor also called about 15 medical students to observe the examination and the severity of my illness. My recollection is that of seeing the doctor in white blouse, nurses in white caps and many faces of younger men around me taking notes of what the head doctor was saying. After that day, I woke up in a large salon with beds on both sides and children sleeping. A nurse comes towards me to give me an injection. This routine was continued for 3 months. I remember that at least every two days the nurse would take me outside under the sun and give me a cold bath and let me sit there for about 15 minutes. With the daily injections and light feeding I began to feel much better. The sight of seeing my father visiting me weekly was like a miracle to me because for him to make that trip from the country to Bogota besides the expense it was annoying and confusing for him to get around. My mother could not visit me once because she was pregnant. Her hope was that my father brought her positive news about my condition every time he visited me. On Sundays my uncle Arcesio also visited me bringing a bunch of bananas every time.

On the second month of my stay in the hospital I was about 75% recovered. I felt much better and to some degree happy. One of the nurses who had a close liking of me asked me one day if I knew how to sing. I joyfully sang a popular song then called," Alla Tras de Ia Montana", Beyond the Mountain.

On the third month I was completely cured, healthy and anxious to go back to Solana to my parents. One Saturday my uncle came to visit me, brought me a safari type suit, shoes and a pith helmet. He dressed me up and said goodbye to the nurses who kept saying that I should go back to visit them some time.

Something new had been added to our household. My younger sibling Gonzalo had been born while I was interned in the hospital in Bogota. Frankly I don't remember feeling emotion about having the company of a younger brother. To me he was just an infant that my mother had to nurse.

Upon arriving in Solana I was given the sad news that my grandfather Nicacio had died. It sounded so unreal to me because before I was taken to the hospital I had spent quite a few moments with him chatting and listening to music made with a hand- made scratchy musical instrument made of bamboo shoot.

At age 6 schooling time began at home. Every day my father would dedicate a few minutes to teach me how to read and write and what a great head start that was for me. At age 7 I was enrolled in the local school. From the start I had the advantage over all the Other children. Their parents did not know how to read or write consequently they could not teach their children and let that task to the school teacher.

In 1947 corporal punishment was then still allowed in the schools. My first traumatic encounter came one day as a surprise when the teacher became upset because we did not remember one of the subjects she had told us in class the day before. She told six of us to stand in front of the black board whipping our behinds with a bamboo shoot. None of us cried but the burning pain remained for a while.

When I told my parents about the severity of our teacher and what she had done to us, my father specially became very agitated. The word of this punishment reached all the parents who in turn complained to the department of education demanding that the teacher be removed. The following week that mean teacher was no longer there and a more gentle and understanding teacher had been assigned to take her place.

After attending 2 years in the rural school in Solana, the teacher conferred with my father about my progress indicating to him that since I was ahead of the other students in my reading and writing, she could not advance me to the next level.

She advised my father to enroll me in the larger school in Macheta where I could move up to the third grade. My father made arrangements with a lady in Macheta to provide room and board for me while attending school. This service was provided to us free of charge. As it was the norm in cases where no monies were involved, my parents provided the lady with a larger portion of the vegetables, eggs, butter and any other foods or fruits above of what my needs were. This arrangement worked very well for us for two years of my schooling. On the third year I was already enrolled in the 4th grade and doing very well.

My Sister Evelia is Born:

When I was about 8 years of age I vaguely remembered that one evening my father picked my brother and I one at a time from the bed we shared and took us to the larger room, spread down a couple of burlap bags on the floor and laid my brother and I to sleep. The time had come for my mother to give birth to my sister Evelia. My mother told my father she needed help and to go and get the mid wife who lived about 2 miles away crossing the properties of at least 6 people. Although there was no horse or any other way to traverse the up- hill terrain in the dark, my father and the midwife arrived in about 45 minutes. By then the yelling of pain by my mother intensified and the baby gave her first cry. I was awake most of the time. My younger brother who at the time was about 3 years old slept soundly.

SCHOOLING INTERRUPTED

On the ill advice to my father by one of my uncles, Sixto, he suggested to my father to allow me to quit school and move to Bogota and assist my aunt Ana in the shirt laundry business she operated. My job was to attend the clients as dispatcher and receiver of the items to be laundered during the day. In the evening I would be attending a vocational school for accounting. Not realizing the unrealistic prospects of becoming an accountant because of the limited formal education I had, my father accepted the offer and the same day I left school and moved to Bogota looking forward to work and to attend school.

Three months had passed and the promises made to me and my father had not been met. This was a disappointment for my father when one day he paid me a surprise visit in Bogota and found me sealing paper bags to package the ironed shirts. He then realized that were duped. He asked me if I wanted to return to school but I felt tremendous embarrassment and felt failure had come over me. I was already 11 years old and felt that I did not fit with younger children in school. I decided to continue working for my aunt with the hope that I would attend evening school, if not for accounting, at least to continue the basic elementary education. One year passed with no prospects in sight to continue some form of schooling.

My father anguished about my future and did not know what to do. In view that as I got older the prospects of schooling were finished and that I should look for another job. That was the time when another of my uncles from my father's side, Arsecio, came to my rescue. He worked as a tool dispatcher at an auto dealership and secured a job for me at the dealership as an office boy. There was not much pay and little future for advancement but at least I was out of the shirts laundry. Since I came to work for my Aunt I lived under her care in her house. Then having the new job at the car dealership my Uncle Arsecio took me to live with him and under his care.

The job as office boy paid me barely enough for me to buy lunch and pay the bus fare to commute to his home daily. I could not contribute any money towards food or rent.For that matter I could see that my stay with him was causing certain amount of financial distress in his family. I admit that my uncle Arsecio had special love for me and the best intentions for my welfare. To realize that nine years before he was the one who took me out of the hospital, bought my first quality outfit, took me home, and now back with him under his care. I felt my deepest love and appreciation for him.

My employment with the car dealership was short lived. After six or eight months, I became ill with flu symptoms. I told my uncle I was returning home to my parents in Solana.

The feeling of despair, hopelessness and shame enveloped me. Upon returning to my parents the only feeling within me was to cry on my father's shoulder and cleanse myself of the shame and failure that even at my age of 13 it was too heavy for me to bear.

In Solana I recuperated my health in no time. I was old enough to appreciate the natural beauty of the plateau and took time to truly take in the peacefulness that exists there. Before dawn we were awakened by the loud crows of the roosters and the chirping of countless birds. Bellowing clouds sit along the highest peaks above the valleys. The crisp clean air suddenly becomes warm as the golden rays of the morning sun erupt over the ridge in the east. The end of the day is indicated by the sound of a soft bellowing wind blowing from north to south as the sun rays disappear over the other ridge on the west.

Living with my parents in Solana was very nice but the beauty and tranquility did not fill me completely for me to remain there. I felt that I was not made to tackle the arduous labor required to make a living and earn a little money. Many at times as I watched my father covered in sweat down to his waist plowing the fields with the bulls I felt such a deep feeling of love and unwavering respect to see him working so hard to make an honorable living. He knew that as much as he needed my help, he would not ask me for it. I in turn offered him to help him lead the bulls while plowing to keep them in a straight line on the furrows. By the end of the day after seven or eight hours of work my legs began to hurt. I just wanted to sit down to rest. I was then convinced that I should go back to Bogota in search of an easier job for me. My father also agreed with my decision.

Just as an act of fate, the following weekend I went to the town of Macheta for Sunday Mass as we usually did. My uncle Sixto, who had previously convinced my father for me to leave school to attend the shirt laundry, came down to let me know that there was a job for me at a travel agency managed by one of his friends. This time I would not be working at the laundry and the job at the agency was full time. This news certainly was a beam of hope for me now that I had reached the ripe age of 14.

Meaningful Employment

As promised by my uncle Sixto, the following day I started to work at the travel agency as a messenger assisting the clients to obtain their passports and other documents to travel abroad. I was earning enough to contribute towards the expenses of the household in my Aunt Ana's home without having to work in the laundry. Having extra time, I did enrolled in an accounting course which qualified me to earn a few extra pesos by assisting an accountant on my spare time. Later I also enrolled in a correspondence school in an attempt to finish by High School. I made some headway but after 2 years I became bored with the classes by mail and decided to quit the program. After 4 years working at the travel agency, I became very interested in learning the English language and took a couple of courses in an evening school. I was already 18 years old and my prospects for advancement in the travel agency was very slim and I felt I needed to expand my future career. I continued to learn a word of English here and there and was becoming more and more interested to live in the United States. The image of the ideal way of life in the states and the personality of the people as portrayed in the movies appealed to me very much. I thought that I could fit perfectly in the American society. I asked myself, will I ever be able to fulfil that dream? I was living from paycheck to paycheck; I had no money.

TRAVEL TO THE USA

My knowledge acquired at the travel agency made it easy for me to obtain the necessary documents and the passport just in case I could travel abroad. I was ready. my break came to me when the office manager of the travel agency said to me one day. "Why don't you go to the United States because there is no future for you in this country." Those words filled me with emotion. I felt my blood rushing through my body as I have never felt before. She further said to me that since her son and daughter were already living in New York they would be my hostesses there. Things started to look promising for me. I further learned that because I was an employee of a travel agency the leading airline Avianca would offer discounted fares to employees of the travel agencies.

For sure, I felt that a new chapter in my life would begin to unfold. With my passport in hand I contacted the United States Counsel in Bogota for an appointment four months down the road. I was told to bring other documents by then. When the appointment time came, I was surprised how cordial they were with me. My original intention was to visit the U.S. as a tourist and I requested a visa for that purpose which was issued in about a half hour's time. Not until later did I realize that I was issued a visa for an "Indefinite Period". I felt that the first door to the United States was opening to me. With my ardent desire to learn English, I purchased a self- taught English book in which I learned approximately 600 words. Not much but it was a good start. I felt already like a well- rounded American speaking English and willing to do any kind of work so long as was legal and my morals would not fall into decay. The time to purchase my airline ticket had arrived. To my pleasant surprise, the airlines asked me to pay only $21.00 dollars for taxes. My father lent me the equivalent of about $350.00 U.S. Dollars which I felt was a large amount for him considering the meager earnings he made from his labor. When I returned 5 years later to repay the loan, he refused it.

Saying goodbye to my parents and relatives, needless to say, it was heart breaking. There is an axiom in Spanish that says: "When you arrive at home it is to live. But when you depart it is to die." My father, in spite of his deep sadness to see me depart, he was very proud to tell everyone in the village that his son Hector was immigrating to the United States for bigger and better things.

Four days before my departure I was contacted by a friend in Bogota, Warner Kajet, who told me that a friend of his, Rudy Kaminski president of a Shipping Company in New York, was visiting some of his clients there and perhaps he could offer me a job. We met on Thursday February 26 1960 and agreed to employ me as a warehouse assistant and for us to meet again as soon as I arrived in New York.

FLIGHT TO NEW YORK

On Saturday March 1, 1960 my host Mercedes Sandoval and I left Bogota to New York via Avianca with a stop in Miami. It was my first experience flying on an airplane in the most advanced passenger aircraft the Constellation with 4 propeller engines. The noise was so loud that the ringing in my ears remained for 24 hours after. The temperature in New York was in the 40's and large amounts of snow packs still remained from the winter months. For me it was a new unfamiliar world and was ready to conquer it. First I must learn the English language. My short term goal was to learn it sufficiently within six months to the point where I could have the freedom to communicate with anyone.

FIRST EMPLOYMENT IN
NEW YORK

On Monday March 2 1960 with my passport in hand
I went to the Social Security Office in the vicinity of
Woodside, Queens. I was surprised that I was issued my
Social Security immediately once the officer verified the
type of visa I had stamped in my passport. On Tuesday,
March 3, 1960 I met with Mr. Kaminski my prospective
employer at his shipping company in Manhattan and my
employment began the next day. So far the lucky cards
had been in my favor and I had skipped the possibility of
me washing dishes as the lowest job I was prepared to take
if the need be.

One month has transpired in my employment at the
Shipping Company, and it was time for me to have all my
documents legal and in order. Although my visa had allowed me to remain in the United States for an indefinite
period, I knew that I needed to obtain permanent residence.
My employer provided me with a letter of intention to employ me for as long as I want it. I also requested a letter
from the local bank indicating that I had in savings at least

$250.00. With these two letters and my passport I went to the nearest immigration office downtown Manhattan. To my surprise, there were only 2 more persons there requesting residency at that time. My application was completed and approved in about 20 minutes followed by the green card sent in the mail to me in about 4 weeks.

Now that I was employed during the day I still had plenty of free time in the evening, I enrolled in the nearest school teaching English in the evening. I was happy because the interaction between the teacher and the students who were all newcomers was what I needed. About a month into the class, the teacher challenged us to write a letter in English to our relatives in our countries to demonstrate what we had learned so far. When the teacher read the letter I had written, she was impressed by it although my formal education in Colombia had been barely 3 years of elementary schooling. She advised me to enroll in Astoria, Queens evening high school where I could finish my high school education. I followed her advice enrolling for the coming sessions in September 1960. I was doing relatively well except in pre-calculous. English was my favorite subject because I had that burning desire to learn lt. I was not afraid of it and challenged myself to learn at least one word every single day.

Of the local newspapers I continually read, the New York Times appealed to me most because of the clarity and seriousness of its reports. I preferred to associate myself with English speaking people as a channel to become part and be integrated in the fabric of society of this country.

MILITARY SERVICE

Two years had passed attending evening high school but still needed another two more years to graduation. My employment at the shipping company working in the warehouse and preparing bills of lading was becoming dull and saw no room for promotion and much less of a future for me. Even though I was treated well, I began to feel anxiety. The time came when I was no longer living with my compatriots. I had found a basement apartment which served my purpose well. In the evening high school I became friends with a fellow student, Fred Mathis, who in turn introduced me to the rest of his family. Fred also began to feel insecure in his job as a bank teller and was in the process of joining the Air Force. After discussing with him the pros and cons I also decided to join the Air Force even though I had not finished my high school. This decision would not come to fruition for me without difficulties during the following two weeks.

The day came for me to enlist in one of the Air Force recruiting offices. Once I signed up my next step was to take an induction test in downtown Manhattan the following day. To my great disappointment I failed the test and I could not retake it until 30 days had passed. I felt deep frustration running through me realizing that I already had quit my job and did not have sufficient money to pay an additional month's rent. I opted to take the train to Connecticut and meet with the local recruiter there. He coached me as to how many questions I must answer correctly to pass the test.

As I remember the test was not difficult but my lack of the English vocabulary had caused me to fail it. This time I felt a surge of confidence run through me and was sure I knew that I could answer the number of correct questions required to pass the test. I felt less pressure this time while taking the test and finished before everyone else with the number of correct answers as required. I felt a sense of relief and was instructed by the recruiter sergeant to report the next day May 14 1962 with my personal items for departure to the Training center in Lockland Air Base, Texas.

Upon arrival at the Air Base the driver who was a civilian drove us to the barracks and in a gentle civil manner told us to take one of the beds and rest for a while. After 18 hours of riding in the bus I was very tired and fell sleep immediately. About 15 minutes later I heard the loud yelling of the sergeant in charge for us to get up and fall outside on the double. I never experienced to be awakened with this type of rudeness before but realized that this approach was the norm while in basic training in the

Military and that from now on there will not be any more gentle commands. I had to accept It without complaint.

The sergeant told us to stand side by side forming two rows. "My name is Sergeant Boggs. You are now in the military and you will always address me as Sir." He told us to do 15 push- ups. Some of us made them with no difficulty. Others slushed to the ground, others who were overweight vomited. It was a depressing site to see and what future would be for our unit. The first introduction by Sergeant Boggs was very effective. Quickly we learned to march, and to maintain our barracks clean, and our bunk beds and foot lockers with our clothes neatly folded. Our boots had to be shiny and our uniforms impeccably clean and well fitted. The First week of basic training passed and was feeling lonely. I began to wonder how or where I could find my friend Fred Mathis who had enlisted in the Air Force one week before I did without stumbling in the entrance test as I did. On the following Saturday he appeared in my barracks looking for me neatly dressed in his khaki uniform. He appeared to be happy and well- adjusted to the military life. He gave me encouragement and to look at the positive aspects of finishing the training which was a must requirement to later have a permanent job assignment. The job to be assigned was firstly depended upon the needs of the air force and the skills demonstrated in the initial test. My test scores indicated that I would be qualified in the aircraft communications and control. That was a surprise to me since I failed the first basic entrance test. In either case, I felt much better after talking with him. It was already June and the hot sun with the high humidity made living there miserable. Of the various field training exercises my favorite time was the weekly hour we spent in the swimming pool, mostly because of the freedom of movement we could have without having the sergeant yelling or correcting us. On the fifth week of training individually we were told what job we would be assigned to for the following 4 years. My future job was to be in the Air Police. As for all job skills we were assigned to a different training school. Some were located in other states and others like the Air police school, was located about one and a half miles from where our barracks had been.

Our sixth and final week of basic training was finally over. Of the 30 recruits who started originally 28 had finished the course. The recruits who were fat, had lost weight and were fit. The ones who were skinny had gained weight and were fit as well. So we all looked much better that day in contrast to the way we looked when we arrived there. The graduation ceremony was much civil with pomp and circumstance in the air. Parents proud of their son's accomplishment attended. In my case I had no one there to congratulate me.

COMMUNICATION WITH
MY PARENTS

More than 2 months had transpired since I had written to my father about my intention of joining the military service, a decision that he would not had been comfortable with. Colombia was going through a civil war practically in every corner of the country. The subject of the daily news there was that of the hundreds of young soldiers who had been killed by the guerilla, and for me to be in the military was a nightmare for him. He did not realize that in the United States there was no civil war and we were enjoying a relatively peaceful time.

My change from civilian life to the military was very traumatic for me. There were too many unknowns in my future and had become neglectful in writing home. Perhaps because I was not even sure if I were to be accepted in the Air Force and what my job was to be, so I let the months go by silenced in my own world. On my first visit to Colombia, 5 years later, my father related to me the anguish he felt in not knowing whether I was dead or alive. He then continued to share with me what he experienced and felt that it was a miracle of God. One early morning still half sleep, he thought and wondered about my fate momentarily. Suddenly he heard the comforting voice of a man saying, "Don't worry, Hector is well." He then woke up feeling a peace he had not experienced before free of and without any concern for my wellbeing. Two weeks after he received a letter from me confirming that I was doing well.

With my basic training complete, I was ordered to report to the Air Police Training School located about one and a half miles away from where we were staying for the previous 6 weeks. My first impression was the large number of recruits was about 200 as compared to the 30 recruits during basic training. With the larger number of recruits we were housed in a larger building while the training classrooms became available. In the mean- time besides doing menial jobs, kitchen duty was on the agenda for almost everyone at least once a week for the following 4 weeks. I dreaded kitchen duty. Just the thought of getting up at 3:30 in the morning to be ready at 4:30 in the respective mess hall made me dislike so far life in the Air Force. Four weeks passed and finally we were told that classes will start the following day. Classroom and field instruction was on the agenda 5 days a week for the following 4 weeks. The environment was more civil and without having to be yelled at by the training sergeants. Time went by fast and the training was over. I was looking forward to know to which air base I would be assigned and was feeling happy to leave that environment once and for all. We were given the final examination test which I though it to be easy. The following day the results were posted and to my dismay my name was not on lt. I had failed the test for academic deficiency. Again, I had to accept the fact that my English knowledge and comprehension was not sufficient. As bad as I felt, I felt a little relief to know that I was not the only one failing. 3 other U.S. born recruits also had failed and had to take the course over again. My sadness was obvious to everyone in my unit. My squad leader about my own age, came to me, cupped his hands around my face and said: "Espinosa, don't be so sad —Sometimes I feel sad too but don't show it." It was the beam of fatherly encouragement I desperately needed which came to me through him on that day. After 4 more weeks my good day had finally come. I passed the test with flying colors and to make the news sweeter I had been promoted to Airmen 2nd class. It was already September 1962 a month later for me, but for the first time since the day I joined in May, I really felt confident that I had made it and was rolling on secure rails in the Air Force.

FIRST AIR BASE
ASSIGNMENT

My first assignment was to the Combat Support Group in Ellsworth, South Dakota. I had no notion of that state but it had to be part of the United States. Finally I was happy to leave Lockland, Texas once and for all. I had figured that the Air Force would pay for my ticket to South Dakota if I flew directly there. However, we were given 30 days leave before reporting to our assigned base. It would be logical to me to stop in New York to visit my friends and spent some time there. That's when I realized that I had to pay for my transportation fares to New York and then to South Dakota. The cheapest way was by bus. Even so, I did not have sufficient money to buy the ticket. Putting my embarrassment aside, I asked about 30 of my fellow airmen to give me one dollar giving them a brief reason for my plight. They all did. From that moment on I began to feel the sense that I belonged in this country and felt special gratitude for the kindness of heart to the people in this country.

Traveling by Greyhound Bus was easy and actually enjoyable. Dressed in my blue uniform I attracted 2 younger girls who probably noticed my shyness and began to engage in conversation with me. Then a few hugs and the kissing came along very easy. From then on I understood and remembered with pleasure the meaning of the song, The Yellow Rose of Texas. What a lovely little adventure it was. Visiting my friends in New York was very nice. Also I learned about the benefits we had available. To my surprise I went to a theater performance "Toys in the Attic" and to a live show by Jimmy Dean both free of charge. Life had changed for the better for me and a sense of self confidence had become part of me finally.

The date for reporting to my new air base was approaching fast for October 2 1962. The bus ride from New York to South Dakota seemed shorter than the time I spent across the State of Texas. After one and a half days I was in South Dakota. The chill in the whistling wind gave me an indication of the severe winter to come in that part of the country for the following 8 months.

I was assigned to the Combat Support Squadron. Because I did not have a security clearance I was not permitted to perform security duty. The estimate time to be properly cleared was to be four months. In the meantime I was assigned duty in non- sensitive nature. The winter blizzards began in early October causing roads and walkways to be almost impassable. I felt of no use and made my superior aware that I had clerical experience where I could be useful but the clerical positions within the squadron were filled by airmen who had been trained in the air force. In the spring of 1963 my clearance had arrived- and was allowed to work as a security guard. I felt trustworthy and was made part of one of the 3 security teams. During the Cuban Crisis President Kennedy ordered the Armed Forces to be on alert status. That meant that the security of the base had to be expanded. Of the normal 8 hour shifts rotated during 24 hours, they converted to 12 hours shifts. It was very tiresome to walk the post for 8 hours alone. After that, the additional 4 hours caused my body to feel numb. Many at times in the early morning I was walking around my post falling into mini sleeps to be awakened by the sound of an oncoming vehicle driven by the supervising sergeant whose job was to keep us awake and alert. As much as I wanted a day time clerical job, I did not mind working at night. The job had to be done whether I enjoyed it or not.

During the middle of the year in 1963 I volunteered for assignment overseas. My first choice was Europe with Japan the second. The Cuban crisis had ended, and the security of the base was reduced to normal. One evening as I was reporting for duty my supervisor told me I was reassigned to work as clerk in the Squadron's Office. My desire to work during day time hours in a comfortable environment had come true. I felt that I had contributed sufficiently by performing one of the less desirable jobs and my recompense was at hand.

Having a day job with weekends off, I ventured with some of my friends to the closest city, Rapid City, South

Dakota and Mount Rushmore where the busts of four U.S. Presidents are encrusted on the rock.

Eight months have gone by working in a pleasant environment. I felt good about my job and the prospects for promotion were coming just around the corner. I was promoted to Airman First Class which meant I was doing my job well.

In early November 1963 I was notified of my reassignment overseas to the Base in Okinawa, Japan. I was looking forward to see other lands and learn other cultures as well. My happy expectations of going overseas were overshadowed by the news that President Kennedy had been assassinated. Everyone was in shock by the unbelievably terrible act. The boisterous mood of the troops prevalent in the base suddenly changed to somber, and laughter was overcome by sadness with a deep sense of disbelief. I felt relief though, that the armed forces were not placed on alert, otherwise my reassignment overseas could have been delayed.

OKINAWA JAPAN

After over 18 hours of lying time the chartered Continental Aircraft landed in Kadena Air Base, Okinawa on the morning of December 5 1962. I felt like a zombie , disoriented, because I remembered I had left California on the 6th of December. How could that be? I had never flown on a transcontinental flight across so many time zones and with so much loss of sleep. The weather was warm and humid which later was the cause of my misery. We were bused to our squadron. As I was signing in the Sergeant in charge said, "Oh, so you are Airmen Espinosa. Your Sergeant from Ellsworth wrote a letter of commendation to the Squadron Commander." Was I dreaming that an airman of my rank be acknowledged? Many of my fellow airmen of higher rank do not get that recognition. I opted to keep it low key but later on it proved to be of immense value to me. Because the base was large and required large number of security guards, I was assigned as member of one of the 3 groups needed to rotate our duty hours to be 8-hours each shift. In addition to the supervising sergeants being friendlier, there were many posts at many locations and we were assigned a different post each tour of duty.

no wind , snow, or below zero temperatures there. There
were many amenities in the Air Base for us to enjoy. The
Mess Hall had civilian personnel hired locally supervised
by the Mess Sergeant. In our barracks there were civilians
who cleaned and polished our boots for a mere 50 cents.
The laundry was within our barracks at very low prices.
A taxi service within the base would run about .25 cents.
The airmen's club on the base served filet mignon dinners
for $1.25 and a drink for .25 cents.

The club was considered a gem for us and to the Marines
who frequented it during weekends since they did not have
such luxuries in their bases. In February 1965 while reporting for duty I was instructed to see our Commanding
Officer Captain Hetzel. I thought, did I mess up in any of
my duties? My desired, but not expected this soon, assignment to work in the office was at hand. I was to work for
one of the 5 Sergeants, Sgt. Corby, beginning the following day. I had thought that the letter of recommendation
from my previous base was discarded or forgotten for that
matter considering the large number of personnel in the
squadron. Again, working 8 hours a day, weekends off and
a pleasant environment where I could wear my locally tai-
lored uniforms. I had it made! And of course was teased
by my fellow airmen for my unexpected success.

BECOMING A CITIZEN

It had been already 5 years since I had immigrated to the United States and was eligible to apply for US Citizenship. I contacted the closets immigration and naturalization office in Guam for an application. I was provided with the application and a booklet to study the laws and government to prepare for the required test.

Normally the naturalization ceremony was performed by a U S Judge once a Year in Guam and I was certain that the Air Force had flights often to Guam and carry members of the military free of charge. I thought of using my accrued leave to take the trip to Guam to be naturalized, but on a casual conversation with my Commanding Officer about me taking a week off, he told me:"You don't need to spend your leave time for that purpose". He called the Base Commander about my intentions and got approval for me to take a week off duty. Special orders came two days later authorizing me the necessary time off, and to be provided with an Air force Vehicle in Guam to do my business as the need be. Everything turned out as planned. I had become a proud citizen of the United States.

The gesture of cooperation given to me by my commanding officer built in me a deep sense of gratitude. I felt that I had contributed so little and yet that contribution as small as it was, was given value and respect to me as an individual.

Back to Kadena Air Base after my affirmation to citizenship my job was relatively easy. I took advantage of the weekend weekly tours offered by the USO to the local villages where living is very simple and peaceful. Some of the villagers were very welcoming and would entertain us by offering tea and some of the local sundries. They had very few material possessions which to an American household would be part of the comforts of living. Yet, to the Okinawans they were not an absolute necessity and lived content doing their daily chores. Working during the day also gave me extra time at night to pursue my High School Equivalence Diploma through extension courses offered by the Maryland University on the base. Once completed the required courses for graduation, I requested the GED from the University of New York which was granted to me. Then I wanted to further my studies through the same University but I did not meet the minimum grade point average which at time was 2.60. I took the classes required increasing my GPA above the 2.60. Subsequently I was admitted in the University for the following 2 semesters until I was sent back to the States. My goals for educating myself further looked more promising. The months went by quickly and by June 1966 my tour of duty in Okinawa was coming to an end.

FIRST VISIT TO COLOMBIA

Having served in the military for 3 years and 4 months upon return from Okinawa to the States, my remaining military obligation would have been less than 9 months. In my case I would had been discharged upon entering California. That presented two-fold problems. I had not visited my parents in Colombia in 5 years and no plans as to where I would settle to look for employment. My obvious option was to extend my military service for an additional 9 months. By doing so, I would have the benefit of being transported at Governments expense across the Continental U.S., then to Colombia at my expense. The plan made sense and put the wheels in motion. Then I was a U.S. Citizen. I obtained my U.S. Passport in Okinawa, then the necessary airline tickets. One at U.S. Government expense across the continental U.S., and the second at my expense to cover the round trip between Miami and Colombia.

The day came for me and was back in the States in mid-December 1965 in route to Bogota to see my parents and the rest of my family. After 5 years of being absent the anxiety on my part was overwhelming. My parents had arrived from the country side 2 days earlier in preparation for my arrival and were staying with my aunt Ana who still operated the shirt laundry.

It was approximately 7:00 P.M., with my expectation of my arrival in Bogota in about 45 minutes I took a look through the window, it was already very dark, but I could see the flickering lights in a village below, the aircraft already descending. Suddenly the engines were placed in full throttle and the Captain gave us the news with disappointment that the airport in Bogota was not safe to land because of heavy fog and we were returning to Panama International Airport. The Captain further said that even though there were other airports within Colombia where to land, the large size of the Aircraft required a longer runway. With sadness and great disappointment we were returned to Panama and housed in a Hotel. After flying for more than 24 hours I was exhausted. My parents, along with 18 of my relatives related to me of the incredible disappointment they felt when they heard the news of the flight being returned to Panama. After 5 years of not seeing me, they imagined that I might not be in that flight after all.

The next morning we departed from Panama at 9:00 A.M. and arrived in Bogota about an hour later. The sun was shining and the gentle crispy air at the airport made my arrival more enjoyable. At that time there were no enclosed gates for arrivals and departures. We disembarked in the tarmac. As I walked towards the gate I saw a group of people waving white kerchiefs at me. Dressed in my blue Air Force Uniform I looked good. I felt very proud to return to my motherland as a U.S. Citizen and member of the Armed Forces. I thought to say to the group of relatives, look, here is your boy from the Village of Solana. My footsteps did not appear to touch the ground but felt like walking on water. Momentarily I sensed my ego going to my head and felt that there was no one else more important than me at that moment. I was the big cheese until I reached the area where passengers are greeted. After 5 years of practically not speaking Spanish, I was tongue-tied but that did not prevent the shedding of tears of joy from me and everyone else.

For the following 28 days in Bogota I was pampered by all my relatives. As I was already in bed sleep one evening, was awakened by the sound of music outside the bedroom where I slept. To my surprise it was a trio of musicians playing for me a serenade composed of the most romantic songs at that time. My aunt Ana was the relative who arranged that event. I thought that perhaps this was the demonstration of her love for me and for her to make amends for having my school interrupted 13 years before Whatever her reason was, I loved it. My first visit to Colombia after 5 years was coming to an end. It truly was an enjoyable time being with my parents, my brother Gonzalo and my Sister Evelia.

MY LAST ASSIGNMENT IN THE AIR FORCE

On or about January 3 1966 I reported to my last assignment in the Air Force. After 18 months of experiencing good weather it was a jolt for me. The temperature the day I arrived was about minus 3 degrees and the snow piles around the barracks were about 10 feet high. My job assignment primarily was to the Security Squadron. My rank and seniority were the reason for me having easier duties and had become acquainted quickly with my new supervisors and fellow airmen.

About 30 days later I was instructed to report to Senior Master Sergeant Gary in the Operations Section. Again I thought, did I do something wrong? To my surprise he told me that my previous supervisor in Okinawa had sent a letter to the Commander commending me for the good job I had done. Because of this I was reassigned to work in the Office of my Commander Officer since an opening was available for me. It was such welcome news for me considering the miserable weather at that time. Again I was working during the day, 5 days a week.

During the month of March promotions were announced. My name was on it with a notation that the promotion to Sergeant was authorized by my previous Commanding Officer in Okinawa. What else could I ask? I was doing very well. However, I was still concerned about continuing my education . Because I already had attended the University of Maryland overseas, I applied and and was accepted at the University of Minnesota in Duluth for the available classes in the evening.

MY FIRST CAR

The university was located about 5 miles from the Air Base and transportation was a problem for me. I was ride sharing but I could not always depend on the driver. The time came for one of the Officers, Lieutenant Woods, to be reassigned to Vietnam in the spring of 1966 and had to dispose of his possessions including his 1965 MG Midget. He offered it to me for $2,250.00 which I thought was a reasonable price. I obtained my first loan from the bank for $1,750.00 plus $500.00 from my own money. With the weather now very pleasant, the little convertible car was a gem for me. I took advantage of the beautiful summer weather driving along the Lake Superior to Canada during weekends. Minnesota has many lakes, and several of them were within short distance of the base, where you can drive and park within 25 feet of the shore and

Enjoy a picnic. So far that was my best time in the Air Force.

The beautiful summer in Minnesota went by quickly, with the fall arriving in early October and the chilling winds followed by the first snow fall for winter. It had been a

year since my arrival in Duluth. In January 1967 I began
to prepare for my discharge from the military on February
26 1967. Although I had enlisted in Connecticut and had
lived in New York, I did not want to go back there. The
cold winters I had experienced for the previous 6 years
made realize that I wanted a warmer climate similar to
that of Colombia. California came to my mind, and without hesitation I decided to drive there. I had my personal
belongings to carry but the MG did not have sufficient
room. Against my wishes and great disappointment I had
to sell the MG for $2,000.00 and purchased a 1956 Ford
Fairlane from my roommate for $750.00. Not the normal
decision to go back to a much older car but it met all my
needs.

The day came for my discharge from the Air Force. I was
reimbursed for my unpaid leave. That came to about
$2,250.00 plus $1,600.00 I had saved through the U.S.
Savings Bond Program. Saying goodbye to my friends was
not easy. They had become like my family. Some were my
mentors who gave me courage when I needed it most. One
of my closest friends was Clinton Bozeman from Mobile,
Alabama with whom I still correspond from time to
time. Once my commanding officer Lieutenant Goldberg,
learned that I was coming to Southern California, he gave
me the name and address of a relative in North Hollywood
who upon my arrival in Los Angeles oriented me and gave
me suggestions as to where I could live.

My options were not many. Not being employed I needed the least expensive housing I could find in a safe area. To the YMCA in Hollywood I went. Very inexpensive and yet it was safe.

FIRST JOB AFTER THE
MILITARY

My skills were limited to clerical work in the military. Still, I had great optimism that I could find suitable employment for me in no time. I dressed myself in one of my tailor made suits I brought from Okinawa and went to Occidental Life Insurance in Los Angeles to apply for employment. I felt that the bigger the company the better chances I had to be employed. I was hired the same day and was told to report the following day at 2:30P.M. to be a supervisor for a crew of about 30 people working from 3:00P.M. until 9:45 P.M. There was also another crew working from 8 A.M. until4 P.M. The job entailed the codification of life and health insurance policies so that the information could be entered into the computer system. I thought that the job was easy and could do it without problems. Coming from the military I was trained to follow orders and directions to the letter. This approach I followed and things seemed to be working well. About 4 months later the sheets of data from the policies was to be entered into the computer system. The computer analysts discovered that the data entered for the same type of policies did not agree and the program would have to be re-vamped. The supervisor of the day crew felt that the shift I was supervising in the evening was making the wrong encoding. She had over 20 years with the Company and the supervisor of the department sided with her. I had to be replaced and reassigned to another department where I had to do a different type of job. I didn't like it and were too many errors on my part. After two days in the new job I was fired. By then I already had moved out of the YMCA sharing an apartment with another newcomer from Florida, Michael Mullins, but my share of the rent and food expenses was higher than before. With the hot weather of summer in July coupled with the asphyxiating smog then, caused my tonsils to be severely infected. I just did not know what to do. I had no health insurance and limited money on hand. I needed to clear my mind at least temporarily but felt that I had reached bottom again. In my frustration I drove to the Santa Monica Beach pacing along where the waves gently reach the shore. I began to cry until I felt relief of the anxiety and insecurity that was consuming me. But the next most important thing was to take care of my health and seek immediate medical attention.

I looked for a medical doctor in the vicinity of Hollywood where I was living. I found a Doctor Charles Lopez on Hollywood Blvd. Although I did not have sufficient mon-ey to pay for his service I took the chance and went to see him. I could hardly speak because of the pain my throat. As I approached the reception area by the window, I did not know what to say because of the embarrassment. When the nurse asked me about my health insurance or what mode of payment I had, I collapsed by the window. Later I woke up with the doctor and a nurse massaging my legs in an effort to revive me. The doctor immediately knew that I had no money to pay him and my embarrassment had caused me to collapse. He told me not to worry, that I could pay him after I got well. His words of encouragement made me feel better. He ordered the medicine for me and told the pharmacist to send the bill to him. My faith in Angels became stronger because that doctor was the representation of an earthly angel who had saved me. Later after getting a new job with health insurance I paid him and even had my tonsils surgically removed by him to prevent further infections because of the heavy smog that blanketed California in those years.

OTHER JOBS

My second job was with a Finance Company making and collecting loans. I worked for them close to 2 years. Collecting past due loans was not my favorite part of the job. I hated it. As the number of past due loans increased I was fired from the job. My experience in this field however, became of value to me and my next move was to apply to the Crocker National Bank in the loan department. Because I had two years of experience in the finance field, I thought I could become a loan officer with one of the major banks in California. I had the gut feeling that Crocker Bank would hire me even though I was fired from my previous job at the Finance Company.

I was truthful in my application and during the interview with the personnel manager as to the reason for my previous demise. She made a phone call to my previous employment to find out if my termination was due to any wrongdoing on my part. About 10 minutes later she came back with a light smile in her face saying to me. "There is nothing wrong with you. Can you start tomorrow?". The respectable job I wanted had come my way finally. And so from May 1969 I remained working at Crocker Bank as a loan officer for the following 13 years.

Having better pay at the bank I could afford to move out of the Hollywood area which had become part of the hippie generation with pot and drugs sold and consumed everywhere. I decided to look for an apartment in the Montebello area which was close to where my job was in Monterey Park, not realizing that I was approaching another fateful stage in my life which made me feel at home.

The inquiries I made for the amount of rents was high for me but I could afford it if I had to. The area in front of the golf course appealed to me very much on a street called Via Alta Mira where I saw a sign for an apartment to share. The building was 2 stories, nicely maintained, with security gate called Villa Yolanda. At that moment a woman was clipping some of the shrubs in the landscaping facing the street. I inquired to her about the other person who was willing to share the apartment. With a broad smile on her face she said to me: "Ask me anything you want to know. He is my son." She went further to introduce herself to me: "I am Yolanda Galli. My husband had named the building after me." The apartment was a 2 bedroom facing the street, very clean, and fully furnished. My prospective roommate was not there. He was up in the mountains skiing so without asking her I assumed he must be close to my own age. And the amount of rent? $125.00 a month. I'll take it. The same day I moved in the few items I had. My clothes, and a few pots and pans in two cardboard boxes.

The following day I met my roommate Ray Galli. He was the same age as I and by coincidence had been discharged from the Air Force 7 months before me. So far the mutual misgivings we had about each other were cleared and out of the way. I also met his father Arthur Galli during the evening hours. During our conversation we exchanged our backgrounds. They had immigrated from Switzerland in the mid -fifties and had gone through their ups and downs just like myself and any other person when newly arrived in the United States. Ray was a wonderful person with me. Although we did not have much in common as to our interests or hobbies, he treated me out to dinner to one of his favorite steak restaurants in the vicinity, and to the Playboy Club where I began to learn and enjoy the good life of a typical bachelor like he was. Many nights he came home very late and in others he did not come home at all. His life style paved the way for both of us not to step on each other's path.

My life was taking a new clearly defined path into the future. A good place to live, had purchased a new 1967 Ford Mustang, had a job with good reputation and dignity and was in excellent health. I thought it was time to reevaluate and plan to continue my education. Having attended the University of Minnesota while I was in the military, the credits were easily transferred to East Los Angeles College where I had enrolled. The college offered sufficient number of classes during the evening and which could be transferred to another university upon completion of the Associate of Arts Degree. That degree normally took two years to complete for day time students taking the maximum number of units. In my case I could not handle the full load of units and needless to say, I was becoming tired and frustrated because of the slow pace and the time I had to spend studying during my off duty time. Many at times, in my frustration I wanted to quit school altogether. The Galli's during that time had taken me under their wings and treated me as their own son and I in turn thought of them as my second parents. They emphatically encouraged me to continue attending College. Not until later years did I realize the value of their timely advice and encouragement.

JOB PROMOTION

By early 1971, I had been working at the bank for 2 years but mostly under the immediate supervision of a more senior Loan Officer. Although my job was to approve consumer loans, there was a certain percentage of the borrowers who for unpredictable circumstances fell into hard times financially and could not pay on time. I had to make the effort to collect those loans by contacting the borrowers. If I could not be successful, the uncollected loans were sent to a central collection department for the appropriate disposition. Within the requirements of the bank my performance was satisfactory. I was then assigned to another branch of the bank in Los Angeles in the area called Lincoln Heights to manage and run my own consumer loan department. I felt good about my new job having a secretary, and an assistant whose primary job was to effect the collection of the past due loans.

The added comfort in my new job, increased pay and the prestige of having a respectable job, did not derail me from continuing attending college in the evening. In that new community soon after I met my first true love who made the most significant change for the rest of my life.

MY FIRST TRUE LOVE

About six months into my new assignment, I had the need to have a document notarized. Because there was no notary in our bank I had to obtain that service from another bank down the street called United California Bank. As I had the document already notarized, I noticed a young girl as a teller who caught my immediate attention. I asked the supervisor what was her name. Oh, she is Margaret her supervisor replied. I thanked the supervisor for having notarized the document and for letting me know that girl's name. I left the bank but I took with me in mind the image of Margaret. It was the simple way in which she had her shiny black hair fall over her shoulders, combined with the lovely and sincere manner of her smile that made her beauty purely sublime.

The following day my assistant told me that while I was out to lunch a pretty young girl had come in from United California bank to apply for an auto loan because her bank did not make loans to its employees. We reviewed her auto application but did not have any credit history and short time employment. Her application was denied.

I had no idea that the rejected applicant was Margaret, the beautiful girl that had swept me off my fee two days before. In the mean time Margaret's supervisor at her bank kept telling her that a couple days ago the loan officer from Crocker Bank was asking for her. That he was a good looking young man and she should make an effort to meet him. She told her supervisor that she had come to Crocker Bank to apply for an auto loan but the only man in the loan department was an older man in his fifties.

On the third day, again I had the need to have another document notarized at the United California Bank and thought to myself, this time I am going to approach Margaret's teller window and introduce myself. I just did that. Without hesitation I asked her if she could see me again, perhaps to go out to dinner. She said yes instantly and a dinner date was set for the coming Saturday night. Ultimately Margaret did get her loan from the credit union where she banked. The date for dinner had come. I dressed myself conservatively but somewhat meeting the style of those days. Blue striped bell bottom pants, gold ruffled shirt and scarf, and proceeded to her home to pick her up. On the front of the house there was a young man about 19 years old washing his car. I introduced myself and the purpose of my visit. I was expecting a cold reception from him considering that I was unknown to the family. Instead, with a sincere smile on his face he said he was David Estrada, Margaret's brother. He made me feel welcome and part of his family.

Ever since, David has always treated me with respect and admiration for what I had achieved in the short time in the United States.

Ironically for my first date with Margaret, I took her to dinner to a classy restaurant at the top of the Occidental Life Insurance Building from which I had been fired 4 years before. The atmosphere was fabulous and the dinner was great. I felt from time to time butterflies in my stomach. Margaret felt the same and did not finish her dinner.

Up to that time I had dated other girls before but never felt that closeness and sincere love as I felt for Margaret. We did not stop seeing each other and went to lunch during our lunch time from work. Many at times our focus was to look at each other and the lunch went practically untouched. It is said that when you are in love, all you hear is music in the air. In my case I heard the music surrounded by the image of Margaret representing herself as a tree covered with flowers. I was madly in Love. If it is not Margaret for me then I'll remain single. Her gentleness and sweet disposition was impossible to ignore. Besides, she had a similar background as mine. Her father, Joseph Estrada, was from New Mexico and her mother Maria de La Luz Estrada was from Mexico. We all had the Spaniard's roots and I was becoming part of the puzzle.

ENGAGEMENT

It was then November of 1971. After several dates I asked Margaret if she was willing to marry me. She said she would. I bought her an engagement ring and set the wedding date for May 20 1972 at the Lady of Our Miraculous Medal in Montebello, California. After the engagement date I got to meet the rest of Margaret's family. Her sisters Dora, Virginia, Louise and of course David who already had given me the okay to be his future brother-in law. It was just about 4 months prior to our engagement that Ray, my roommate, had decided to marry. He moved out to a home he had purchased on his own. The Gallis decided to move me from the 2 bedroom apartment into a one bedroom apartment with reduced rent in exchange for my helping Mrs. Galli do the chores in the building. I enjoyed very much living in that unit on the second floor overlooking the swimming pool below and the view of the Montebello Golf Course.

THE WEDDING DAY

The wedding day was approaching very quickly. The Gallis had made the necessary arrangements for practically everything. The special day for us had arrived, May 20, 1972. Margaret looked beautiful in her white dress. She had her hair curled and lightly resting on her shoulders. During the ceremony her little nervousness was overcome by her beauty and her innocent and welcoming smile. The wedding party with all its splendor included the flower girl, the boy with the ring, the maid of honor, the bride's maids and the best man. The reception was offered and prepared for us by the Gallis at their residence in the Villa Yolanda. I was surprised by the number of people attending, close to 60 I recall, considering that no one from my family in Colombia attended.

After the reception we departed for our 2 day honeymoon at the Madonna Inn in San Luis Obispo, give or take, 200 miles north of Montebello. About 15 miles from Montebello we were hungry and stopped for lunch at a pizza place in Toluca Lake. We both felt relaxed looking forward to the drive and check in at the fabled Madonna

Inn. The Madonna Inn proved to be a unique place for honeymooners. Painted in pink outside and inside the main entrance and the restaurant, and each room with a different decor and motif. Our weekend honeymoon was short and sweet, but we had to return to our respective jobs on Monday. On our return home we did visit the historically famous Hearst Castle which was and is located by the route towards Los Angeles.

Margaret moved in with me in Montebello but was no longer working at the bank in Lincoln Heights. So her traveling time to work took her over 20 miles one way and through much heavier traffic. Luckily she found another job closer to Montebello at a Savings and Loan where she worked in the Escrow Department. Things were falling into the right places.

During the first few days of being married and living in Montebello, Margaret felt home sick. She missed her parents, and the companionship of her sisters. It just broke my heart to see her cry but there was not much I could do. She had to overcome that sad feeling of being separated from her family. Soon after she learned to accept the reality that she was not going back home. The critical period of adjustment after marriage was coming easy. Our goal was to wait about 3 years to start a family. In the mean time we should travel and visit the places we wanted to see.

On one occasion we went to Las Vegas along with Victor Diazgranados who was my best man in our wedding and his wife lsa, both from Colombia. Victor had been working at the same bank branch with me and had become good friends. Our first stop in Las Vegas was at a casino where we all eagerly began to gamble and play the slot machines. Margaret asked me for $5.00 to play Keno. To our surprise she won $1,100.00 on the first game which Margaret and I used later to buy the airline tickets to Colombia for her to meet my parents for the first time.

TRAVEL TO COLOMBIA AFTER WEDDING

The first trip to Colombia with Margaret and I was stunning for her. She had never been on an airplane before, much less visiting other countries in South America. At the airport we were received by My Brother Gonzalo, my sister Evelia and of course my aunt Ana who was the connecting party between Bogota and the rest of the family in Macheta. We were driven to my aunt's house where we stayed while in Bogota. She no longer had the shirt laundry, instead she had a large house rented where she provided room and board to students. My brother Gonzalo was working as a computer programmer for IBM of Colombia.

The next day we traveled by bus to Macheta with my brother. The road to our village, Solana, had not been built yet and of course there was no electricity either. Margaret for the first time had to travel by horse lent to my father from his brother. I had to go on foot. From the town of Macheta to Solana the road goes down into a canyon then it begins on an uphill on the opposite side until it reaches the plateau of Solana. The trip took approximately two hours considering Margaret's lack of experience horseback riding, the pace was slow. As for me the sight of Solana filled my heart with deep joy. The place where I was born and had lived until the age of 12. Neither of my parents went to Bogota to receive us in preparation to have the house cleaned. My father by then had an extra bedroom and a bathroom built in preparation for our arrival.

However, the village like all others had no electricity as yet. My father had no idea how Margaret looked or where she was born, neither my mother. But in spite of that they fell instantly in love with her. Her sweetness and her profound sense of humility reached deep into my father's heart.

The countryside in Solana was an unforgettable experience for Margaret. The croaking by the roosters in early morning and the chirping of the abundant number of birds made us get up and enjoy the crisp air before sunrise. Later on the day chores had to be made and Margaret was there along with my mother and brother; feeding the chickens, milking the cows and picking up the eggs from the nests. Just like a child on the first visit to a farm. Three days in the country had passed quickly. Again, Margaret traveled to Macheta on horseback. She was not as afraid as before but the horse sensed her inexperience riding and at the first sight of fresh corn along the road, the horse veered up and over a boulder fence to take a quick bite. That was an experience that Margaret would never forget.

She did not fall off the horse and was not hurt. That episode surely showed Margaret's unyielding courage.

Back in Bogota to my aunt's house, we were able to do some shopping and visit some of the most attractive sites in the city. At that time my brother Gonzalo and my sister Evelia also came along. Over all, the trip was wonderful and full of experiences and memories to remember.

BACK IN THE USA

By the spring of 1973, having attended East Los Angeles College for 3 years, I had completed the requirements for my AA degree and promptly applied and transferred my credits to California State University Los Angeles. My enrolling there was very important for me but I did not realize then what ups and downs I was to travel and how long it would take before I achieved my dreamed graduation. Cal State does still today offer a full curriculum in the evening for many career majors. That was very encouraging to me. At first I selected Business Administration as a major and enrolled for 3 classes with a total of 12 units. In that quarter I did perform satisfactorily. As the classes became more demanding requiring more off duty study I had to reduce my enrollment to 2 classes to keep my grade points up. In my desire to move faster towards completion of my degree I changed major to Real Estate since the market in those days looked promising. I took just about all the classes required for Real Estate when the market began to crumble. I had to restart my curriculum to Business Administration and take some of the classes I had skipped before. More work and added anxiety.

By the spring of 1975 I was still attending Cal State University with a long number of units needed for graduation. I was getting tired of school and again I felt like quitting school altogether. The Gallis continued to be our second parents. They had us over for dinner very often with Ray and his wife Micky as well. Ray had discontinued his college and was already self- employed in the textile business doing very well. When I commented to them for the second time my desire to quit school, they were vehemently opposed. I must continue, that someday with perseverance I would receive my diploma. Their encouragement kept me going, quarter after quarter, and my credits became larger and larger. I was already about a third done in credits towards my degree.

By early summer in 1975 Margaret became pregnant with our first son Hector Hugo. We were still living in the one bedroom apartment. It became obvious that it was not practical for us to continue to live there. The Gallis told us that one of the 2 bedroom apartments was going to vacate in about three or four months and for us to move in as it became available. Again, the rent was reduced so long as I continue to help Mrs. Galli with menial chores.

The day came for Margaret to give birth to our first son, Hector Hugo. He was born on June 1st 1976 at the Beverly Hospital in Montebello, California. It certainly was a day with a special significance since it was the bicentennial of the United States.

BIRTH OF OUR SON

With the birth of our son our lives took a new path. Margaret decided to quit her job to be a home mom and in particular because she wanted to breast feed the baby. Not having prior experience the breast feeding turned to be not as simple as she had imagined it. With trials and errors without success she turned for help to an institution called "La Leche". In a matter of two days the baby was able to feed sufficiently and without frustration for both the baby and Margaret. Things were looking very good. Both Margaret and the baby were in good health and by then we had moved to the 2 bedroom apartment across from where I had previously lived with my roommate Ray. This apartment building also was built about 20 feet above street level and had a very nice partially shaded view of the street below and the golf course. That was to be our home for the following three years.

As our son grew the need for an appropriate living environment for him became a must. At that time we had to walk him about one half mile to the nearest park, so he needed a grassy backyard where he could play and have more freedom. The real estate market was slow but there were plenty of homes available within our budget.

My job at the bank was secure and the employees were offered mortgage loans at 1 percent below the standard rate and no escrow processing fees. It was the time to put our wheels in motion to explore whether we could afford a home.

BUYING OUR FIRST HOME

In the spring of 1979 with the help of a real estate agent, the first day we were canvassing the area of Rosemead about three miles Northeast of Montebello, we found what we were looking for. A 2 bedroom house which needed a few things repaired and a general cleanup. The price was $55,000.00, and with a loan of $50,000.00 with payments of about $375.00 a month, it was workable within our budget.

The help given to us by Crocker Bank made it possible for us to buy our home. The time had come for us to begin to pack our belongings. Pack and move to our own home? It seemed like a dream to be in the path of fulfilling the American dream of home ownership. Just to think that 10 years prior when I moved in with the Gallis all my belonging were a few dishes packed in two cardboard boxes. But that day I was moving out with my family and two truckloads of personal property.

LIVING IN OUR NEW HOME

Once we moved in our son who was almost 4 years old showed his happiness without restraint. There was an ample yard in the back with a large shady tree where he had me set up a swing, and plenty of grass and loose dirt to mix it with water to give himself a cherished mud bath. Once we were settled it was time to get to know the neighborhood along Artson Street with the houses freshly painted and neatly maintained lawns, I said to Margaret: Now that we moved to the suburbs, let's go out and take a walk. She thought it to be very funny since we had moved barely 3 miles away.

We were settled in our new home but it would had been nicer to have an additional source of income. Margaret thought she could take care of about 3 or 4 children during the day to supplement our income. She obtained the day care license from the State and was caring for up to 4 children at one time for almost a year.

Having her day care license, Margaret then applied for a full time job at a day care school called Gerber's Children Center; our son Hector would be attending the same school free of charge. That arrangement certainly helped us to put our finances in balance.

PLAN FOR CHANGE OF JOB

The year was 1980 and Crocker Bank was going through a major change. A feeling of insecurity came over me and I thought it was time to look for another employment. During the past two years the bank had made an agreement with State Farm Insurance by which the agents were referring their clients to the bank for auto loans. I was handling the program and had become friends with several agents who impressed me with the professional manner they conducted themselves and their insurance business.

I thought to myself that I saw myself as an Agent for State Farm very comfortably if it was possible for me to be part of that group. Some of the agents had suggested to me to inquire further with the local manager because I was the type of person who fit the profile they were looking for. I got cold feet and decided to continue working at the bank with the hope that things might change for the better. To my surprise the Vice President of the Bank had promoted me to Assistant Vice President which besides the respectable title it did provide me with a pay increase.

The job stability at the bank appeared to continue with promising returns for the following two years, but I could not discard the possibility of becoming an agent for State Farm. In the spring of 1981 ,I met with the local manager of State Farm wanting to know more about their program of becoming an agent. The first item for me was to write him a letter requesting my appointment and what my strengths were to be utilized as an agent. He also gave me a booklet to prepare myself to take the State Insurance Licensing. Once I had met all the requirements the appointment would be mid- year in 1982. By then I would had been 13 years employed by the bank and eligible for some percentage of my retirement pay. The prospects for a new career had begun.

Preparing for a change of career was challenging because Margaret was pregnant with our second child Viviana. The pay for a newly assigned agent was meager for the first two years and again, there was the possibility of not being appointed at the end of the 2nd year. My home had equity and thought to get a line of credit for about $15,000. In case I needed it. It was a good decision.

VIVIANA'S BIRTH

Viviana was born on December 10 1981 at the Monterey Park Hospital in Monterey Park, California. Being our second child things were much easier specially for Margaret who had to carry the larger portion of the load, and the baby grew up and developed without any problems .

GRADUATION FROM UNIVERSITY

In the middle of 1981 after attending California State University for about 8 years, I was finally eligible for graduation with a major in Business Administration. After 2months since I had applied for graduation, I received a letter from the Graduation Department that my curriculum was missing a class in microeconomics and for that reason my request was denied. In my disbelief, I wrote a letter to the Dean requesting that I be given credit for my prior work experience in lieu of the microeconomics class missing from my record. By then I had worked in the Finance Company and Crocker Bank for a total 12 years. After the dean read the letter which I had personally handed it to him, he said: "Who told you about this procedure?" I told him that it was of my own doing. He further said, at least you have your own mind and initiative. He approved my graduation request and ordered the clerk to issue me a Certificate of Graduation. It truly felt like one of my biggest achievements to date. For the time I spent at California State had become part of my existence. Walking back I did not feel my feet touch the ground. Success at last. I knew then that my father dreamed that at least one of us could had earned a degree but he did not have the funds to help us pay for it. I mailed him a copy of the certificate which he held in his hands for a long time in disbelief to know that one of his dreams had come true.

NEW CAREER

By the early spring in 1982 I already had obtained one of my insurance licenses and began to prepare for the second license. In addition to the licenses for insurance, State Farm preferred that the prospective agent had finished college. In my case as I had commented to the manager previously I was about two quarters away from my projected graduation date from California State University with Business Administration as my major. In March of 1982 we were in the planning stages as to in what community I would be opening my office and what expenses I would incur.

Again, a flashing opportunity came about because one of the senior agents could no longer perform his duties as an agent due to an auto accident he had, besides he was in the process of retiring at any time. The area manager of State Farm asked me if I was willing to move into his office and service his portfolio until it was distributed later with other agents. The secretary from the retiring agent had over 5 years of experience in the insurance business and had agreed to remain employed. For me, not having any insurance background other than what I learned obtaining the license, it was like asking me to jump into an icy river to see if I could swim it across. In spite of my fears, I agreed, and proved to be the best decision that channeled me into a rewarding career.

The expenses for rent and salaries were covered by State Farm for the first two years. However, my starting salary was $425.00 a month, barely enough to cover my mortgage payment. The rest of my expenses were met by income Margaret received for providing child care at home. The financial stress we felt did not deter me from the goal that I was going to succeed and become an agent two years down the road. On one occasion while shopping for groceries my son Hector, who was 5 years old then, asked me if I could buy him a $2.00 toy he saw in the store but I said no. May be another day if I could sell a life insurance policy for which I would receive commission. Every day when I came home day after day he asked me: "Dad, did you sell a policy today?" I felt my heart break then and his words remain with me until the day I die. Running the insurance office with my limited knowledge was challenging but not impossible. I was learning more and more every day to the point that some of the customers asked me from what Insurance Company I had come. My work days extended many at times until late at night. I thought that no matter how small the policy was it had the potential to become many more policies from the same customer or from his referrals.

The first year at State Farm I spent it mostly learning the ins and outs of the insurance business. The pressure was mounting on me because I was not selling enough life insurance and was performing at a lower level as compared to the other newly hired agents. In the early part of March 1983, the manager and I had a meeting. He was concerned about my poor performance especially in selling life insurance. Yet, I had shown that I had sufficient knowledge on the subject. He said, "Why don't you like to sell life insurance?? That question was like an insult to me because I liked to sell it but had not truly made the push for it. At that moment, I felt a surge of energy in me and said to him. "You will need to fire me because I'm not going to quit." He replied, "That's what I wanted to hear". I further told him that by the end of August I would have sold the 20 life policies required to be sold for the entire year.

With my mind made up I focused myself on selling the 20 life policies by the end of August 1983. I elaborate on this experience because it taught me once again a lesson that nothing can be accomplished until the person has the ardent desire to do it. Having met the insurance sales goals during 1983, State Farm did approve the Independent Agent contract with me on the second year. I was saved and felt that I had crossed the icy river to dry land. I was assigned part of the portfolio of the retired agent, and was entitled to receive commissions on all policies I sold plus the ones assigned to me. Even though I was then responsible for all the expenses of the office, when I received my first pay check I thought I had won the jackpot. I had plenty to pay my office expenses and, in addition, bought that new car my son had pointed out to me with the International Flags on the side. By then my son didn't want that $2.00 toy any more. He wanted a Nintendo Game.

SCHOOL YEARS

By 1984 our son was enrolled in Saint Anthony's Catholic School in San Gabriel, just a few blocks from where we lived. Margaret was working again at the Gerber's Children center and Viviana in preschool as well. Margaret always strived to expose our children where they could learn new things and become confident with themselves. She enrolled Hector in the local youth soccer league which requires involvement with the parents. Margaret volunteered to be a soccer mom which requires a great deal of time of her part. I was not there as I should have. My goal was then to grow my insurance office and much of the time I spent it selling insurance. In my mind I was looking down into the future when Hector and Viviana were ready to go to college and be able to provide the wherewithal for them. Margaret did say to me many at times that she wished I was there. That sentiment in her began to get bigger and bigger until it came to haunt me in later years.

With the Spanish language in our background it would have been obvious to many of our friends that we all should be speaking Spanish at home but we weren't. I was completely convinced that we should speak English at home, and the goal for our children was that English was the primary language for them as well. Perhaps because of the difficulties I had in my previous years for not mastering the language, I didn't want them to face the same obstacles. In that respect, I admit that I had learned enough English to guide my children whenever they needed help.

One occasion I was walking to church with my son, then 8 years old, and in casual conversation I addressed to him with a compound sentence which I thought to be very difficult at his level but there was no answer required from him. The following Sunday as our routine was, we were walking to church chatting. He then addressed to me in a compound sentence and with a different subject.

At that moment I knew that Hector was listening to me and was learning the importance of learning the English language well, and later it proved to be one of the key factors for him to become a lawyer.

FAMILY TRIPS

As a family we made a few trips usually within California. One of them was to Yosemite National Park, Catalina Island, and of course, Disneyland and the San Diego Zoo. A trip to Colombia was made in mid 1986 with the 4 of us. Viviana was 5 years old and Hector 10 years old. The time was appropriate for my parents to meet their grandchildren grown up. The excitement for my parents to see them was twofold. Seeing that their roots were extending to a foreign land, and that the children spoke only English. Even so, they managed to communicate with each other rather well. The novelty that my two children whose father was born and grew up in Solana were speaking in a foreign tongue spread around the entire village. Suddenly we had an unusual number of neighbors coming to visit us with the excuse that they wanted to hear my children speak with each other. But how is that possible? Some of them commented with surprise and admiration. Besides the neighbor's curiosity, my son and my daughter were surprised to see how the house looked and where our bedroom for the evening was to be. My son could not wait and had to have an immediate tour. Seeing the attic that my father made of corn stalks tied by hemp to store the corn where the mice night after night came to feast, he climbed up the 6 steps on the ladder my father had made with sticks of wood, his curiosity had paid off. I never imagined it like this, he said. The roosters began to croak at about 4 A.M. and continue until 5:30 A.M. at which time both children got up to feed the chickens. Hector got to become friendly with one of the large crested roosters with gold plumage, but to his disappointment and sadness, it was the one we had for lunch the following day.

Viviana in turn, became very friendly with one of the white chickens and insisted she wanted to eat the eggs from that chicken only. I did feel that the trip to Solana was easier than in the previous years. The road had been built and we had traveled by bus. After so many years of waiting for the electricity, the whole village had been electrified by then. It was finally a step into a more civilized world; the radio and television had finally come to Solana.

Back in the United States from Colombia life continued with the normal routine of taking the children to school. Margaret still working at the Gerber's Children Center with Viviana attending Pre-school. In my insurance agency I had my share of problems in selecting and keeping the right employees just like any other business. In all, I was doing well considering the competition for insurance. I must say that once I had the personal contact with a customer he or she usually remained loyal to me even if our insurance prices were higher than the rest of the companies. Some of those customers remained until they died, and some stayed with me for the 25 years I had the insurance agency.

PURCHASE A NEW
HOME/HECTOR BEGINS
HIGH SCHOOL

By 1991 my income had increased considerably and we were in need of larger home. Even though the market was at a high point we found the home that was right for us in San Gabriel a little over 3 miles from Rosemead. Hector had just began High School and would have preferred to attend the public school in Rosemead locally, but Margaret and I felt that he should continue his schooling by attending a Catholic High School in La Canada, about 19 miles from San Gabriel. Hector was not happy to attend that school so far away from the local environment and having to leave his friends from Rosemead. Four years later he realized the value of attending St Francis High.

During his Senior Year at St Francis, Hector and his class were taken to a 3 day retreat that was new to him and to us. Upon returning to campus they were told to meet in the school auditorium that evening unaware that the parents had been asked to be there as well. Each student had to give a short speech about the experiences they had in the retreat. When it was Hector's turn to give his speech, Margaret and I were totally mesmerized by the professional manner he put the audience at ease by starting jokingly relating how he selected that particular retreat which was the most expensive from the others less costly. We were filled with joy and pride to see our son how he had matured before our eyes and felt that the tuition cost and the extra effort we had made was worth every penny.

In 1993 Viviana had been attending St. Anthony's Elementary School which entailed joining the Girl Scout Brownies. Besides the effort and time needed for Viviana to sell so many boxes of cookies if she was to earn a trip to Disneyland, Margaret was there with her at all times.

There were overnight field trips and hours and hours spent by Margaret to make sure Viviana achieved what she was supposed to. I was not there. Margaret said to me from time to time that there was one of the fathers with his daughter in whatever event they had. I thought that Margaret was better suited to help and assist Viviana during her outings for that reason I left that chore for her to do. Was I right or was it just an excuse for me not to help her?

HECTOR TO THE UNIVERSITY

After the many applications Hector sent to different Universities he was pleased that UCLA had accepted him. It was a relief to me because I knew that the tuition was reasonable and could easily pay for the entire four years. The time was coming when he would leave home and live near campus.

One day as I was in the freeway to see a client, I saw our van driven by Hector and packed with his belongings in the way to School. I then realized he had become independent and I did not have to help him. He had taken it upon himself to pack and be on his way as a responsible young man. Like many new students, Hector did not have in mind what his career major would be at UCLA. Because he had been acquainted with our dentist, I suggested to him to pursue a career in dentistry which would provide him with a good income. It sounded good for the time being. During his second or third quarter at UCLA he was required to volunteer at a local Hospital near campus. He called me one evening and his voice sounded with fear and disappointment to tell me that he just could not stand the sight of blood anymore and that he did not want to be a dentist after all. I said to him, son, don't worry. Pursue the career you feel comfortable with. He was concerned because by changing majors he would loose at least 2 quarters. Again, I was sympathetic and understanding with him and not to worry if he lost one or two quarters of study. He chose to major in Economics, and after decided to attend law school.

VIVIANA ENTERS
HIGH SCHOOL

In 1995 Viviana had finished her Junior High School and based on the sound education provided her at St. Anthony's, we thought for her to continue her High School at Ramona Convent High School at a short distance from our home. It was a very good school just like most Catholic Schools that provide good academics and the good old plain discipline. Margaret continued to keep vigilant with Viviana's progress in school and had her enrolled in the local girls' soccer league. That meant more and more demands placed on Margaret to be a soccer mom. My only assistance to her was to be present during the games which of course I enjoyed very much.

Financially I was feeling the strain having to pay tuition and housing expenses for Hector, plus the tuition for Viviana's school. That left us with hardly with any disposable income. Just about at the same time, the office building I was renting for my insurance agency came up for sale and a new feeling of insecurity began to torment me. That office had been used as a State Farm Office for over 30 years, so moving for me was out of the question. Luckily the owner and I came to an agreement for me to buy the building and of course my monthly outgo had increased. I then proceeded to use the equity on my home to secure a line of credit to give as down payment for the building. The decision to buy the building proved to be valuable then and in future years. My tight budget situation had relief mostly because the auto insurance rates had increased, so my commissions, based on the collected premiums, also had increased.

HECTOR GRADUATED FROM UCLA/ATTENDS LAW SCHOOL

In 1998 Hector graduated from UCLA with a major in business/economics and decided to attend Law School. Again, more applications submitted and plenty of uncertainty to come. The best choice of school was at the U C Hastings College of Law in San Francisco. His departure from Southern California left a deep vacuum within us and a feeling of uncertainty since he had to depend on student loans for the first year .Not until his last two years he was awarded scholarships to help him reduce the debt. On his third year of law school a law firm from Los Angeles recruited him to work upon his graduation. Further, the law firm paid for the extra classes he needed to prepare him to take the BAR Exam which he passed in the first examination.

MY FATHER'S DEATH

In 2002, while Hector and Viviana had vacation time from school, we took a trip to Colombia to visit my parents. Margaret did not go because she had been recently employed and did not want to jeopardize her job. I could see in my father's features that he had aged rapidly. My mother began to have one of her legs swell as a result of early stages of diabetes. My father was still very capable of taking care of the animals and doing lighter work in the farm. As we said goodbye, I had the sense that it was the last time my father and I embraced. About 30 days later my brother called me to let me know that my father had become very ill with cancer in the stomach. He died a week later.

The passing of my father was devastating to me. I felt that the union I had with him miles away had been broken finally. I then realized that even myself past the age of 60 I was not ready to accept the inevitable. He will live in my heart for as long as I exist on this earth.

MY MOTHER'S DEATH

In the year of 2005, my mother could no longer ambulate because her leg became very inflamed. She was hospitalized but the doctors saw that the only possible way to extend her life was to remove the entire leg which was by then affected with gangrene. The operation was performed and within 2 days she died.

VIVIANA GRADUATES FROM HIGH SCHOOL/ ENTERS UNIVERSITY

In 2000 Viviana graduated from Ramona High School and began the usual routine that most High School Students go through. Again, applications sent and hope that she is accepted at the University of her choise. Well, she did get accepted at the University of California in Santa Cruz. Again, the tuition and housing was within our budget to handle. On the third year she was given the opportunity to study abroad. She accepted, and decided to study in Spain for 6 months. I then thought that the Spanish culture was perhaps what she needed to comprehend the meaning and value of certain rules of behavior we had tried to instill in her but which had been ambivalent to her. During the first six months, Viviana communicated to us that she was very happy studying in Spain, and had traveled to Portugal and England. Further, she told me she had a meeting with one of the School Deans and was advised that if she wanted she could remain there for another year, getting full credit towards her grade at UCSC, and that the tuition and room and board would remain the same. That was another opportunity for her to learn more of the Spanish culture and should take advantage of it. Margaret and I were happy to have Viviana study in Spain for another year.

During the following year in Spain, Viviana traveled once more to England and to 3 cities in Italy. All I knew of her travels was the charges she had made on the credit card I had given her for emergency expenses. Later she related to us the adventures she encountered, some of which were very risky.

The year was 2005 and the school year in Spain had finished. Upon return to Los Angeles, I picked her up at the Airport. Soon after in the way home she said to me: "Dad, now I understand you." Those words spoke volumes to me. I was so glad I encouraged and supported her when she needed it .Viviana graduated from UC Santa Cruz in Latin American Studies as her major .Then she attended San Francisco State University for the following three years earning her degree in education in 2007. During this period she met Alan with whom later she contracted matrimony.

RETIREMENT

In 2006 I was approaching retirement and a year earlier I had notified State Farm of my intent to retire effective December 31 2006. I had the necessary income for Margaret and I to take the trips we wanted to take and enjoy our retirement in a relaxed manner since there was no need for her to continue working at the Pharmaceutical Company where she had worked for 4 years. The office building was going to be sold as well to supplement our income further.

On May 20 2006, the day of our wedding anniversary, while having dinner at a restaurant she told me that she did not want to continue our marriage and was moving out in a few days. I thought that what she had said was directed to someone else but to me. Margaret leaving me? Impossible. After 31 years of marriage, and having worked for 25 years in the insurance business to prepare ourselves for the golden years, it was unthinkable. I begged her not to leave; just tell me your conditions you want and I'll abide by them.

She said no, her decision was final. In a few more days she began to move out some of her belongings, then I realized that during all those prior years while she was involved raising the children and she needed me, I was not there. My assumption was that she knew why I did not helped her, and that she was supposed to be strong. I did not pay attention to her and had lost that loving care I had in the earlier years. I even suggested to her for both of us to see a marriage counselor but to avail. Our marriage was over and I had to learn to accept it.

Once I accepted my marriage's demise I tried to take trips here and there in an effort to at least make me forget that Margaret was no longer with me. I always felt the vacuum for her absence and anything I did with my life had no meaning any more. Some of my friends suggested I meet other women so I would not feel so lonely. It was not in my character and my morals to meet other women outside of my marriage. I had made a promise before God, friends and her family that I would marry her for better or for worse until death do us part. Besides, I could never face my two children, who I love so dearly, with another woman.

Our agreement was for us to continue living apart. I was to pay the rent for her apartment, and other expenses for her health insurance, auto insurance premiums, gas for her car, plus other miscellaneous expenses as they occurred. Besides she was still working earning sufficient money for her to have a comfortable living. I continued to remind her that the doors to our home were open at any time she decided to come back. I still have hope that some day she decides for us to be together again. Financially, it would benefit both of us. My retirement from State Farm was 3 months away. I asked Margaret if she wanted to join me for the last event in my career on December 16 2006. She said she would, but a month before the dinner event she changed her mind. It was another great disappointment for me. I felt terribly embarrassed with my superiors and fellow agents if I showed up at the event alone without Margaret being with me When I commented with my son Hector my latest disappointment . He said, 'Dad, don't worry, I'll come with you." That evening at the dinner he gave me a hand written letter he wrote congratulating me on my retirement realizing my humble beginnings from the Country in Colombia, and wished me well on the trip I had planned to take to Egypt. That trip I could not take after all because War had erupted in that region.

After 31 years of marriage living by myself was not easy to become adjusted. But as the days and weeks went by, after one year I began to accept my fate. First of all, from day one, it was not in my character to become vindictive with Margaret. The opposite, my attitude was to live separate lives but in a cordial environment, even though many at times she showed some anger whenever we met. I fully understood that the anger she felt towards me was the result of the accumulated wrongs I had caused her in the years past, and which she had kept to herself.

Time heals so long as no new injuries are caused by either party, and our relationship has become friendly with mutual trust and respect for each other. Many at times I invite her to our house for dinner or to go out shopping without any discord. Faithfully, every year I congratulate her on her birthday and during the Christmas season, we all gather at either our house, or at my son's or our daughter's house and exchange the Christmas gifts. In that respect we continue with our most cherished traditions.

Even though ultimately I have learned to live alone, I still have hope that Margaret will come back to me, and with open arms I will receive her, because I still love her. The mother who gave birth, cared and loved my two children. That fact cannot be erased or forgotten, and spite of being separated from me I realize that the flowers have fallen but I will continue to water the tree.

HECTOR'S MARRIAGE

On June 20 2009, our son contracted matrimony with Stephanie Henderson. There was some similarities with me in the manner they met but had ended with different outcomes. I became familiar, to a certain extent, with Margaret by declining her auto loan application while both were employed at different banks in 1971. While my son Hector was taking applications from the Law Graduates at Loyola Law School for possible employment at the Law Firm where he worked, he became very interested in Stephanie's background and subsequently she was hired. A year or so later they got married.

The wedding and ceremony was held at the Laetitia Winery in Paso Robles, California, in the outdoors with shaded trees and in view of the vines surrounding the winery and the honey mooners hideaway Chalet. That too was an overnight honeymoon like ours. Later they took trips to India, Argentina and Brazil.

Our son's marriage was certainly a big event, and it would had been appropriate that my Brother Gonzalo and my sister Evelia be present. As it had been in the past years the main problem was their lack of funds, even though I had offered my brother to pay all costs if he wanted to come to visit me in California he declined my offer for one or more excuses. My sister on the other hand enthusiastically said she would come but was very concerned that a visa might not be granted because it was extremely difficult to get one. I wrote a letter to the U.S. Counsel in Bogota requesting a tourist visa for Evelia explaining who I was and how long I had been a U.S. Citizen. My sister was given the visa the same day of her appointment with the counsel.

TRIP TO EUROPE

In June 2011 Viviana had the desire for her and I to take a trip to Europe since I previously had commented to her my desire to visit Spain in particular. She further suggested for us to visit London as well. She made all the booking arrangements in no time and away we flew on our first stop to London.

With over 1000 years of history, there is no shortage of museums, sites and historical buildings to see. What we needed was more time. With barely two days overlay, the first place we visited was Buckingham Palace and the timing was perfect to witness the colorful change of the guard during the queen's jubilee. The Parliament building, Big Ben, the London eye and the famous bridge where the London Tower sits, plus plenty of walking along the River Thames. It is an impressive city to anyone who visits it. But for me the most memorable item was the scrumptious English breakfast we were served in our hotel. Our next stop was Barcelona, Spain. The casual and unhurried way of life is immediately noted everywhere. The primary goal of the Spanish people is to enjoy life first, then work but not too much.

The most important site we visited was La Sagrada Familia's cathedral which was started before the civil war and continued by Gaudy. The cathedral's design is like no other in the world. The casual walk down Las Ramblas which ran approximately for one mile with restaurants of every kind every 100 feet and shops to find anything the person wants. Our next stop was Madrid. From Barcelona to Madrid we traveled by train, and what a pleasant ride it was with its spacious and very comfortable cabins running at about 100 miles an hour for the most part.

Madrid is a very impressive city with its massive buildings, immense statues, and the wealth accumulated from the Spanish conquests is ostentatiously displayed. Madrid is not only for the wealthy. There is plenty of shopping to be done for anyone's budget. In our case, Viviana found two pair of leather boots and she could not depart without them.

Viviana wanted to show me where she lived while attending school in the vicinity of Cordova. Of course, I wanted to see where she had spent the money I had sent her while in school.

The great relationship I have with Viviana has allowed me to continue to travel with her. Any time she has extra vacation time left she just asks me, Dad let's go somewhere. Recently we took another trip to Portland, Oregon to see and enjoy the green scenery surrounding the mountains with its crystal clear water falls that empty into the colossal Columbia River. To my surprise my son at the last minute, who has been there several times, joined us there. The quality of food, the clean air environment, and the relaxed atmosphere in general, makes it an ideal place to clear your mind and release the frustrations of daily life.

VIVIANA'S WEDDING

Viviana married on July 3, 2010 in San Juan, Puerto Rico to Alan Somech born in Puerto Rico. They met in San Francisco while Viviana was attending San Francisco State University. From the earlier days of dating she felt that she had met the right man to share her life with. Alan in turn felt that he finally had met the girl of his dreams and would not renounce her for anyone else. He was working as an investment analyst and advisor and his future was promising.

In December 2009 during the Christmas season, Alan and Viviana took a trip to Puerto Rico for Viviana to meet his parents. She felt and became part of his family from the moment they met.

The wedding ceremony and reception was held at the Hotel El Convento in San Juan which dates back since the Spanish had control, but now it was turned into a charming hotel shrouded in history. Everyone was in a cheerful mood. Margaret and I, in spite that we were separated danced, to our heart's content.

The trip for me was a morale booster and in particular to see my daughter lavishly enjoy her wedding day. After the reception, Alan's parents invited me to stay with them for a few more days which gave me the opportunity to see the rest of the island while enjoying the cooking by Alan's mother and that of the locals as well.

One of the benefits of being retired is the freedom to travel and to visit relatives. Since 2007 I have made several trips to Colombia to visit my brother and sister. During each trip my heart is filled with melancholy as I reach the plateau in Solana and see the white roofed house in the middle of the village where I was born. With the house empty, a flashback of my youth appears momentarily, but only the memories of my father and of my mother remain. The squared parcels of land, some green, some brown, and some fallow give a sense of the continuity of life in the village by the new generation.

During 2013 I also had the opportunity to take another trip to Israel and Italy in a pilgrimage through my church. Early in the year the plan was to include travel to Egypt but this segment was canceled due to war in the region.

In Israel we visited all the sites relating to the life of Jesus Christ from his birth to his death. It truly was for me one of the most important aspects of my life as a Catholic because it gave me a more in depth understanding of my religion. But not all our visits to the different sites included religious ceremonies. In the Sea Of Galilee we went on a boat fishing where Peter the apostle fished. We caught no fish, but the sound of the local Jewish music playing in the boat made it irresistible and the entire group spontaneously holding hands began to dance and sing until we returned to the boat dock again.

The second part of our trip in Italy began in Rome where we stayed two days. The first visit was to St. Peter's Basilica with its breathtaking grandeur, should be seen at least once by everyone. We visited also the Coliseum ruins, famous fountains and other tourist attractions.

In general Rome has maintained a charm that delights anyone visiting. The outdoor cafes and restaurants with their relaxed atmosphere is coupled with the incomparable taste of their pasta dishes. On the third day our pilgrimage continued traveling south by bus towards Bologna with a stop to visit the Cathedral of Father Pio in St Giovanni Rotondo where his body lays inside a glass enclosure. The following day we proceeded towards Bologna where we stayed 2 nights. One of the side trips included Venice where we spent almost all day sightseeing the city surrounded by water with its gondolas cruising the canals. It truly is a city of charm and romance. One of the advantages of going on a pilgrimage is the opportunity to meet and enjoy the company of your fellow travelers. The time spent traveling by bus leads everyone to be at ease in conversation and, as it was in our group, singing practically at all stages once we had departed to our next destination.

MY FIRST GRANDSON

On March 6 2013, the third year after Hector and Stephanie had married, my first grandson Evan Hugo was born. He brought joy to everyone in both families, and became the center of attention for my son Hector and my daughter-in-law Stephanie. For every decision it was no longer "the two of us", because Evan had tipped the scale on his favor. I saw my son's attitude and demeanor change from that of the adventurous traveler to that of being a father with a definite purpose in his life. Stephanie who was well prepared to be a mother became the nurturing mother with hands on from the very beginning. The time had come for Margaret to have her wish fulfilled: to take care of Evan daily while Stephanie went to work. With her love and experience bringing up children it was no difficult task for her. It was an eye opener for me watching her take care of Evan, being aware that a child even from an early age understands and begins to learn from what we do and what we teach them. Frankly, I don't remember being that keenly aware how my two children developed in early childhood, perhaps because I was too busy focused to achieve my financial goals.

CONCLUSION

I conclude by saying that my life mirrors somewhat to the action and effect to that of the Kite Runner: First, the struggle to raise the kite to the desired flying height, then by giving it gentle pulls to keep it afloat. In my case, however, my falls have not been gentle. From my early years in Colombia with no vaccinations available then, I was struck with Chicken Pox, and measles. Then, I almost drowned in a pond; struck by a bull; and the most serious illness, diphtheria, from which I miraculously survived.

Having achieved my goals in the United States I am content, and forever I will be thankful to every person who has extended a helpful hand to me. I'll always have in memory my deepest appreciation for the loving kindness that Mr. and Mrs. Galli provided me during a crucial stage in my life. Both have passed away.

If there is something I wished I could have done differently, is that to have better communication with my wife in all aspects of our married life, and by giving her the love and support when she needed it most.

Finally, I feel now have reached the crescendo in my life with gratitude to the United States. With pride I can say that, after 54 years, I have met my quest to learn the English Language sufficiently for me to be able to convey to my readers my own story: "From the Horns of the Bull to the USA."

ACKNOWLEDGEMENT

I like to give my thanks to my publisher, Outskirts Press, for their professional advice provided to me and their efforts that made it possible the publishing of my book.

Hector Espinosa

CPSIA information can be obtained at www.ICGtesting.com
Printed in the USA
BVOW11s1047230215

388660BV00001B/1/P